YOUR KNOWLEDGE HAS VALUE

Susanne Richter

Critique for the Open Source Development Model

GRIN Verlag

Bibliografische Information der Deutschen Nationalbibliothek:

Die Deutsche Bibliothek verzeichnet diese Publikation in der Deutschen National-
bibliografie; detaillierte bibliografische Daten sind im Internet über http://dnb.d-
nb.de/ abrufbar.

Imprint:

Copyright © 2005 GRIN Verlag GmbH
Druck und Bindung: Books on Demand GmbH, Norderstedt Germany
ISBN: 978-3-638-80717-3

This book at GRIN:

http://www.grin.com/en/e-book/75567/critique-for-the-open-source-development-
model

GRIN - Your knowledge has value

Der GRIN Verlag publiziert seit 1998 wissenschaftliche Arbeiten von Studenten, Hochschullehrern und anderen Akademikern als eBook und gedrucktes Buch. Die Verlagswebsite www.grin.com ist die ideale Plattform zur Veröffentlichung von Hausarbeiten, Abschlussarbeiten, wissenschaftlichen Aufsätzen, Dissertationen und Fachbüchern.

Visit us on the internet:

http://www.grin.com/

http://www.facebook.com/grincom

http://www.twitter.com/grin_com

Seminar "Open Source Software Engineering"

Winterterm 2004

Critique for the Open Source Development Model

Susanne Richter

25.02.2005

Abstract

This paper will show the problematic aspects of Open Source Software by looking behind the scenes and unveiling its mask of a happy and satisfied world of cooperating hobby-programmers with an enormous creative potential.

Contents

1 Introduction 2
  1.1 Disambiguation 3
  1.2 History of Open Source Software 3

2 Strengths of OS 5
  2.1 Open Source Definition OSD 5

3 Weaknesses of OS 7
  3.1 Problems and Limitations 7
  3.2 Conflicts Among Developers 9
  3.3 Pseudoproblems 11
  3.4 Death of an OS Project 13

4 Legal Questions 14
  4.1 Warranty 14
  4.2 Announcement of Source Code 14
  4.3 Development and Payment 15
  4.4 Leasing 15
  4.5 Allocation for Download 15
  4.6 Patent Right 15
  4.7 Licenses 16

5 Examples 17
  5.1 Unix 17
  5.2 GNU 18
  5.3 Linux 18
  5.4 Costs Example 19

6 Conclusion 20

1 Introduction

You can hardly find another topic moving the software world more than the dispute between Open Source and Commercial Software [End00]. You can simplified describe the following positions.

First Open Source promotes developing software in non-industrial organizations or during a bureaucratic process but through spontaneous cooperation by interested people who don't have any business relationships. Second, users are said acquiring software not only in form of object but to insist on the source code. Third, Software should be preferably given away. And Fourth, Software should be given away without any protection of copyright or license [End00].

Glass, an American observer of the software scene, wrote that he didn't understand two facts about the open source movement: programmers lovely read anybody's code and people work for others without getting paid. But there are more understanding problems with this new cult. When you look behind the mascots and easygoing sayings then questions about the main assumptions of this field of activity come up [End00].

A very famous paper named "Cathedral and the Bazaar" from 1999 described open source development model as a bazaar. The author Eric Steven Raymond wrote: "I believed that the most important software (operating systems and really large tools like the Emacs programming editor) needed to be built like cathedrals, carefully crafted by individual wizards or small bands of mages working in splendid isolation, with no beta to be released before its time. Linus Torvalds's style of development release early and often, delegate everything you can, be open to the point of promiscuity came as a surprise. No quiet, reverent cathedral building here rather, the Linux community seemed to resemble a great babbling bazaar of differing agendas and approaches (aptly symbolized by the Linux archive sites, who'd take submissions from anyone) out of which a coherent and stable system could seemingly emerge only by a succession of miracles. The fact that this bazaar style seemed to work, and work well, came as a distinct shock." [Ray99]

He showed OS as a magic solution [Bez99]:

- Open source is a progressive phenomenon (bright future of mankind) with no problems.

- The best open source projects employ the so-called "bazaar model".

- Microsoft should be destroyed.

- All software developers are moving towards the "gift economy" in a "post scarcity society".

- The open source movement consist of ideal cooperative people. Conflicts are few and can be resolved within a community.

- Like a primitive society the movement is (successfully) regulated by unwritten norms and taboos.

That sounds so amazing that I wonder why not every software is developed during an open source software process? Later on this paper will show that reality isn't that simple.

1.1 Disambiguation

Open source wasn't the whole time the title for what this paper is about. The turn-around from free to open source software took place in the already mentioned paper "The Cathedral and the bazaar". In his versions until 1998 Raymond uses the expression "free software", after it was replaced by "open source". The word free is not only ambiguous (like free beer and free speech) but also a little bit dirty. Free Software was formed by Richard Stallman, the founder of GNU movement. Its devotees still keep this term alive. Officially, Open source became the new name during OSI foundation meeting in February 1998. Reason for this meeting gave Netscape's decision to lay open the source code of their browser. After this historical step the computer and financial press used the new term "open source". Devotees of free software still criticise that "open sourcers" would only focus on pragmatical aspects, usability, features, reliability and the efficiency of software. They would disregard beliefs like freedom, community and other principles. "In fact, that's the genuine difference between these similar terms: free software follows a political philosophy and open source software is a development model." [Gra02] Stallman says the following sentences when he categorises software: [hSI05]

> "The term open source software is used by some people to mean more or less the same thing as free software. However, their criteria are somewhat less strict; they have accepted some kinds of license restrictions that we have rejected as unacceptable. We prefer the term free software"

1.2 History of Open Source Software

Let's have a short look on the short history of OSS.
Software was delivered as free adjunct with new computers until middle 60's. Manufactures made exclusively money of hardware. Source Codes were freely available for all enthusiastic programmers in the whole world. First 1965 IBM finished delivering source code together with operation systems of computers. At the beginning of the 70's several programmers assert making much money out of their own developed software. With the aid of license contracts narrowing or even restricting dissemination of software from one user to another they protected their sources of income. Source Codes became the best kept secrets of young businessmen.

Almost ten years later Software was developed behind closed doors. In this way manufacturers could retain control of their tools. Non-Disclosure-Agreements bared programmers from free enhancements their products.
Richard Stallman from the MIT and the later founder of Free Software Foundation was so unsatisfied with this evolution that he decided in 1984 to reproduce a free software package named GNU. His aim was the recreation of open co-operation among software developers to benefit for all computer users. Moreover Stallman created GNU General Public License (GPL) protecting the freedom of software.

The word "free" let the economy become quietly sceptic. That gave Eric S. Raymond 1998 reason to propose naming software together with open source code in the future Open-Source-Software. The Open Source Definition says nothing about using open source software among commercial software. [Gra02], [Ber05]

2 Strengths of OS

The strengths of OSS result from its primary aims: developing software in non-industrial processes and so on. In the internet you can read what the official homepage www.opensource.org says about basic ideas of open source: "The basic idea behind open source is very simple: When programmers can read, redistribute, and modify the source code for a piece of software, the software evolves. People improve it, people adapt it, people fix bugs. And this can happen at a speed that, if one is used to the slow pace of conventional software development, seems astonishing."
The main advantages of open source are the following [Ber05]:

- Source Code is optionally extendable, improvable and individually adaptable.

- Bugs and security holes can be fastly detected.

- Permanent quality improvement of software.

- Independent development and continuity of software.

- Less expensive than commercial products.

- Usage of open standards guarantees compatibility and portability

2.1 Open Source Definition OSD

Bruce Perens wrote the first version of OSD with the name "The Debian Free Software Guidelines" and improved it adding messages from a lasting for months email conference. Open source developers should follow the 10 criteria of the Open Source Definition [htt05]

1. *Free Redistribution*
   The license shall not restrict any party from selling or giving away the software as a component of an aggregate software distribution containing programs from several different sources. The license shall not require a royalty or other fee for such sale.

2. *Source Code*
   The program must include source code, and must allow distribution in source code as well as compiled form. Where some form of a product is not distributed with source code, there must be a well-publicized means of obtaining the source code for no more than a reasonable reproduction cost preferably, downloading via the Internet without charge. The source code must be the preferred form in which a programmer would modify the program. Deliberately obfuscated source code is not allowed. Intermediate forms such as the output of a preprocessor or translator are not allowed.

3. *Derived Works*
The license must allow modifications and derived works, and must allow them to be distributed under the same terms as the license of the original software.

4. *Integrity of The Author's Source Code*
The license may restrict source-code from being distributed in modified form only if the license allows the distribution of "patch files" with the source code for the purpose of modifying the program at build time. The license must explicitly permit distribution of software built from modified source code. The license may require derived works to carry a different name or version number from the original software.

5. *No Discrimination Against Persons or Groups*
The license must not discriminate against any person or group of persons.

6. *No Discrimination Against Fields of Endeavor*
The license must not restrict anyone from making use of the program in a specific field of endeavor. For example, it may not restrict the program from being used in a business, or from being used for genetic research.

7. *Distribution of License*
The rights attached to the program must apply to all to whom the program is redistributed without the need for execution of an additional license by those parties.

8. *License Must Not Be Specific to a Product*
The rights attached to the program must not depend on the program's being part of a particular software distribution. If the program is extracted from that distribution and used or distributed within the terms of the program's license, all parties to whom the program is redistributed should have the same rights as those that are granted in conjunction with the original software distribution.

9. *License Must Not Restrict Other Software*
The license must not place restrictions on other software that is distributed along with the licensed software. For example, the license must not insist that all other programs distributed on the same medium must be open-source software.

10. *License Must Be Technology-Neutral*
No provision of the license may be predicated on any individual technology or style of interface.

If any software follow these 10 criteria, then you can call it open source. These criteria create the strengths of open source software.

3 Weaknesses of OS

"Experiences is a wonderful thing, it enables you to recognize a mistake when you make it again."

Because Open Source Software is a development model, it has its own set of problems. Application qualification has to be verified in every different field of application. There are several questions needed to be answered: technical questions like "Does the chosen periphery support open source software?"; and economical questions like "Can you really save money using Open Source Software privately or commercially?".
Just until a few years, Open Source was only popular to insiders. And today someone has to ask if there exists a open source solution for its application area. In Germany the project "BerliOS" by the Federal Ministry of Economy and Technology shall produce relief . BerliOS has to act like a neutral arbitrator between users, developers and support companies with main task of showing which open source solutions are available or should be developed.
For each open source software package we have one developer or a group of developers committed to making that package the best it can be. If a project has a bug, the developers responsible for it wants it not have bugs. But the reality is not that simple. There are popular papers revealing that weaknesses of OSS projects fall into three primary buckets: management costs, process issues and organizational credibility [Bez99]. This section will present different problems which could surprise the reader.

3.1 Problems and Limitations

DOES OPEN SOURCE REALLY PROVIDE A RAPID DEVELOPMENT ENVIRONMENT?

"Open Source does work, but it is most definitely not a panacea...Software is hard. The issues aren't that simple." Jamie Zawinski

Jamie Zawinski developed the Netscape Navigator and took part in many other OS projects.
OSS is made by developers being widespread all around the world. Ordinary projects have the advantage of meetings and face-to-face communication. But these meetings are impossible for OSS programmers. The only way to communicate is provided by the Internet. But Internet has one big error: missing development advantage. When programming work requires everyone to develop on a single and fixed task, the pace of OS development became slow or even slower than traditional projects. For Example, TeX was fully created without the medium Internet.
At the same time there are counterexamples that grandiose projects are created by small groups of developers. They are more productive than a large community, this inhibits innovation. The more developers involved the worse their cooperation is and projects even may stagnate. If there exists developer A who is interested in finishing the project

quickly than he may have the problem of missing authority. Developers work for fun and they don't like being commanded around. A has to wait until every important developer worked at his part. Speed in a project can only be reached through authority. People have to do their task persistent. But authoritarian methods kill any given project and they militate against each OS principles. So, when speed is important you need authority. In history of Open Source Software the best example for authority or even "cult of personality" is the Linux project with its "guru" Linus Torvalds. One developer has a tremendous amount of authority and this centralization dissatisfied developers which frequently lead to several splitting competing projects.

To answer the question if OS really provide a rapid development environment, you can loudly say no. It provides no speed but quality and simplicity.

WHICH IMPACT DOES THE TOWN COUNCIL EFFECT CAUSE?

"Show me the source" (Linus Torvalds)

Alan Cox, developer of Linux kernel, also named Town Council effect "The committee for the administration of the structural planning of the Linux kernel". So what does the Town Council effect really mean? You can say, that is a particular bureaucratic superstructure of developers. Programs aren't produced in isolation. Many users with email play an important role, they want to take part in the project and change its directory of development. But often majority of users have more dangerous smattering and opinions than helpful ideas for the code. Therefor a core team like a clique is created. Now every code changing must nodded through this core team. This of course seems undemocratically, but for the project it is en essential fended position that only a small group effectively work for the project.

The Town Council effect contradicts the OS principle that everybody can change the source code non-restrictively.

IS THERE A SIGNAL-TO-NOISE-RATIO OF E-MAIL CONFERENCES AND SUPERSIZED EGO PROBLEMS?

"To succeed in the world, it is not enough to be stupid, you must also be well-mannered." (Voltaire)

Although this quote is much older than the Internet, it describes Internet communication very well. You can find a lack of cooperation, decorum and useless things. It's much easier to express hostility, selfishness and simple nonsense in emails than in a face-to-face communication. As already said, OS doesn't own the ability of these (natural) things. Internet just isn't the ideal way to communicate although it connect so many developers. But often they rather use Internet for fanatic diatribes against "The Others" than for solving operations system errors or similar problems. For Example

devotees of BSD or Solaris make shrill exchanges: "It ill be a cold day at the equator before Linus Torvalds sets aside his ego for the sake of someone else's better ideas." [Bez99]
To answer the current question, you can say yes and an intelligent and rational communication through Internet is almost impossible.

3.2 Conflicts Among Developers

THE PROBLEM OF THE "LOWEST HANGING FRUIT"

> *"Blessed are those who have no expectations, for they will never be disappointed."* (Buddha)

A successful project always dependents on the interests of developers. Their personnel interests and tasks to develop "cool" programs are the most important drive for the success of project. Not rarely projects die because the initial developer lost interest and nobody pick up the work. I must admit developing projects without interest make no sense. But on the other hand it's a great pity that many projects never reach version 1.0 just because nobody no more wants to work for it. Even less incentives and insufficient quality of feedback can keep a project afloat as long as there exists interests of developers. [Bez99]

FRAGMENTATION AND NIH SYNDROM

> *"The 'free source' Unix-derived world seems to be suffering from exactly the same kind of fragmentation and strife that occurred and is still occurring in the commercial world."* (Dennis M. Ritchie)

The author of this quote is employee at Bell Labs since 1967. He worked together with Ken Thompson and others the first time at the project Unix.
What the quote is about is a symptom for the fundamental problem: the tragedy of commons. That means for OSS that many people work at the same issue and they all own it after finishing. But inside these people there exists the human desire of building clans and make it better "than the stupids". They want proudly show their membership and wear colors of the clan. This desire very often leads projects to splitting in orthodox groups with other own names. In these new groups members practice NIH: Not Invented Here which means that code from competing groups cannot be good and everything must be written new and of course better. The reason beside mentioned desire are polymorph. Very often dissatisfaction with the management (or Town Council Group) is reason for a split. Today there are too many non-compatible Linux distributions like Red Hat, Suse, Caldera, Mandrake or Slackware meaning that same functionality exists

several times but cannot be used together anyway. You can say that Linux definitely suffers from a personnel disorder.[Bez99]
On the other hand Open Source movement becomes some kind of a "religious war" and it's driven by ideological and technological disputes. The competition between different splitted groups also can be seen as a drive for the projects.
This behavior delivers their collective enemy Microsoft an important advantage. In general, commercial software holds one single standard for their products. So they can guarantee users total software compatibility.

BIAS TOWARD POWER USERS

When users have questions about commercial programs they have the possibility to use support service. OSS isn't commercial, so it has no paid people taking over support. In this situation projects and their future direction are dominated by the most technically savvy users. Of course this fact makes OSS attracting for professional programmers in academic and research environments. [Bez99]
This fact makes OSS also undemocratic. Those people understanding the most issues of a project govern its development.

CRITICAL MASS PROBLEM - DOES WINNING MEANS STAGATION?

"Nothing in the world can replace persistence. Talent will not [..] Genius will not [..] Education will not [..] Persistence and Determination are omnipotent." (Calvin Coolidge)

Calvin Coolidge was the 30. President of the United States from 1923 until 1929. The meaning of this statement for OSS is similar to the problem of developers loosing interests in projects.
If there is no critical mass of developers, then soon the project belongs to history. The depleting of developers negativly effect the most viable projects. But great amount of working people for a project isn't right, too. I have mentioned it before : the bigger a company is the more uncreative its work is. There is a small driven group missing. For Example Netscape. At the beginning of company history the employees wanted to work to make their company successful. After it was, they wanted to work for a successful company. What I wanted to say was that lasting success unmotivates. Maybe people leaves current project for other exiting jobs which means the danger of loosing critical mass.
OS project is in danger when it's very successful. It could stand still. Developers must be more persistent. But often they aren't so.

CULT OF PERSONALITY, BURNOUT OF THE LEADER

"Never in the field of human conflict was so much owed by so many to so few."
(Winston Churchill)

Open source may sound democratic, but it isn't. I have already mentioned that sometimes there exists a cult of personality. Leaders of the best-known open source development efforts often explicitly stated that they function as dictators. For Example, if Linus Torvalds doesn't like the changed code, there is no other way than abolishing the changes.

In the beginning of a project a determined and dedicated leader is very positive for the project. But later on when quality counts more than only dedication it often comes to burnout of the leader. The capacities for coordination a project by one single person won't suffice. And if the project earns success, work for the leader grows up so high that he cannot handle it anymore. The burnout is near. [Bez99]

It's useless to exert pressure on the developers. Because of that they mutate to employees but they want to work for fun without any pressure.

Cult of personality like Linux can probably lead to burnout of the leader and may effect the dying project.

MICROSOFT AS A VITAL PART OF THE OSS MOVEMENT

I couldn't believe that in fact Microsoft should be a vital part of the OSS movement. But sure, a great community with same passion and goals often has a collective enemy everyone can hate. With Microsoft OSS movement has found its own political program or even agenda, let's call it ABM/BTM (Anything But Microsoft/Better Than Microsoft). That means that Microsoft's solutions are never good enough and you should prefer other solutions that are better. [Bez99]

Through this agenda a war mentality "We Against Them" was created and it isn't just a funny game. OSS developers really believe and live after this mentality. They don't recognize that they are loosing focus and drift to competition on desktop and server with Microsoft.

This, let me call it childish, behavior of OSS devotees draw off the attention from real aims of open source software.

3.3 Pseudoproblems

I've already shown some problems occurring in OSS. But there are still some which actually are not really problematic.

OPEN SOURCE IS IMPORTANT TO PROGRAMMERS ONLY

Is this sentence true? And if yes, is it really tragic?

Sure it's right that the majority of Linux users don't have the skill nor the motivation to add anything to OS process. For them access to source code is the ultimate documentation and so usability increase. They use Linux like Windows: install and then wait for new versions or improvements.

I wonder why not. There is a mass of developers who are skilled to change code and they work for those projects. Other users without these skills needn't think about possible improvements. They just use what others develop.

IS OPEN SOURCE IDEOLOGY "UTOPIAN BALDERDASH" LIKE COMMUNISM?

This statement was made by Bob Metcalfe who worked at ARPANET and the first Ethernet by Xerox. And the first answer to him should be: Open source provides an alternative you can take or reject.

You can admit that OS resembles Marxism in some views. The key component of Marx work was that companies should belong to those who work for it and that wealth should distributed equally among the workers. There is a great difference between theory and praxis of communism. Several more or less radical directions of Marxism exist and OSS as western social democratic parties follows the moderate direction with most momentum.

Well, OSS has the task of balancing between publicly available knowledge and proprietary for-profit knowledge. And you can't totally compare OSS with communism like Bob Metcalfe did.

TECHNICAL SUPPORT FOR OPEN SOURCE IS INFERIOR IN COMPARISON TO COMMERCIAL SOFTWARE

This sentence would implicate that commercial software support ist good. But the opposite is true. Customer support is more and more saved and vendors cannot afford technical support. The situation has gotten so bad that companies are springing up to supply support for a fee.

So you can say that commercial software support is so bad that this advantage is on side of OSS.

OSS PROJECTS ARE LIMITED TO PROJECTS THAT ARE BASED ON EXISTING PROTOCOLS

Standards and prototypes are an important advantage for distributed Internet-based projects. But OSS projects aren't completely dependent on those technical things. They can afford to be simpler than commercial software. For-profit software must offer a real property advantage for customers. They have to be so complex that they cannot be copied easily. So, complexity is an more or less advantage of commercial software.

OS software prefer using standards but they aren't dependent on them. Simplicity is an advantage of OSS.

3.4   Death of an OS Project

Open Source is not a magic bullet ensuring success. In this branch there exists a high mortality rate. Unfortunately many projects never reach magic version 1.0.

BURNOUT

The initial leader of a project overworks because of a just too different task. He often never more or less finished first version which could keep developing by interested other developers.

INABILITY TO ACQUIRE A CRITICAL MASS OF USERS

Even if a project was completed successfully there is the danger that other just grab the code, develop it in another direction and all initial endeavors are destroyed. Developers and so the critical mass leave the project which means its uselessness and thus death.

LOSS OF THE LEADING DEVELOPER

It could happen that leading developer begin another work and has now no more time for the current project. The project is now missing the drive and will probably stand still. Another reason I also mentioned before could be that the leading developer suddenly loose interest in project.
When the "chief developer" is distracted by anything especially healthy incidents it kills the project.

FORKING

Because of ego-related infighting forking which means parallel different tasks often lead to death of the project. Mostly a lack of organizational and diplomatic abilities of the leading developer is responsible. He mustn't rip the power over other developers.[Bez99]

4 Legal Questions

The use of OSS is connected with engaged discussions about praxis of distribution an application. Of course OSS can be copyrighted if the changed program shows individual characteristics. The famous GNU General Public License can only be applied properly under copyright.
This section tries to explain the most important legal question about Open Source Software.

4.1 Warranty

A frequent objection of Open Source Software is the missing warranty and thus missing secured application of the software. Even GPL No.11 includes a caveat emptor. And sure, the model of making available the Open Source Software would break down if there existed a worldwide warranty claim. Moreover it's impossible to identify the authors belatedly or if you can, they don't own enough resources for warranty. So what to do with OSS? From judicial point of view, the abandonment of OSS equals donation. A donation is characterized by a missing commitment of payment. But donation right would require a notarial certification which is absolutely impossible for OSS. The donor is the initial developer and he remains this position and grant the use rightevery following user in the chain of dissemination. Donation Right doesn't provide any rights to warranty, amendments or additional delivery. That's the reason why a contractual caveat emptor like No. 11 GPL is taking effect.
One thing still needs to be discussed. If one developer passes OS programs over renumeratedly, the buying right must be used. So the consumer has the claim of warranty and removal of defects. Damages is possible if the seller maliciously concealed a certain defect of the product. [Koc04]
As we can see, warranty is a complicated legal question of OSS. But developers have to provide warranty exclusively in case of selling their products.

4.2 Announcement of Source Code

There exists the question whether every single code changing has to be made available when this software fulfills GPL?
GPL No.2 instructs that making available becomes first necessary through dissemination of source code together with its changes. Users have an actionable claim of announcement of code changes. [Koc04]

4.3 Development and Payment

Sometimes professional programmers develop OS software. But the problem is that they work for payment even if they do this in their free time. According to the law of originator, all patent rights of software which was made by employees, belong automatically to the employer. A possible solution could be that the employer only pay for the working activity itself and not for granting right of use. But the employer cannot acquire the complete position as originator. From this legal position the employer now can dispose the software to the Open Source process. Before and during the development the software is not open source. [Koc04], [hSI05]

4.4 Leasing

Leasing is a kind of payment and thus lead to prohibition of leasing right through GPL. Anyway, not every form of ASP (Application Service Providing) is forbidden. For example, a provider of web services may make available just the functionality but not a certain exemplar of program. [Koc04]

4.5 Allocation for Download

The right of making available someone's code is not regulated in GPL. In No.2 GPL says only "copying, distribution and modification". American right includes also online transmission with the term "distribution". But European right separates the distribution via Internet or through data medium. So, based on GPL developers are not allowed to make their code available. But sure, nobody can afford the shipping of data media with programs. [Koc04], [hSI05]
At this point, OSS needs desperately call for action. GPL must be completed by the term "making available".

4.6 Patent Right

Patent right has the aim of publication inventions and developments with the effect of encouragement of technical improvement. It's important at software development that intellectual property is protected. This fact is mirrored at the licenses.
The developer Victor Yodainc first patented Realtime Linux. But software in Germany is copyrighted and there exists no possibility to patent it. Many companies tries to by-pass these prohibitions by patenting software together with hardware as technical unit. These Software-Patents are extremely risky because of the danger of trivial patents. It means that more and more simpler algorithms are patented and and thus endanger developers. They could infringe a patent unwittingly. [hSI05]

This situation inhibits development of OS software and existing innovative potential leaves unused. In his way, patents miss the point.

4.7 Licenses

This Paper doesn't want to explain the differences between the several licenses because other papers concern with this subject. I just wanted to mention them.
The table below shows the most famous licenses and what they provide.

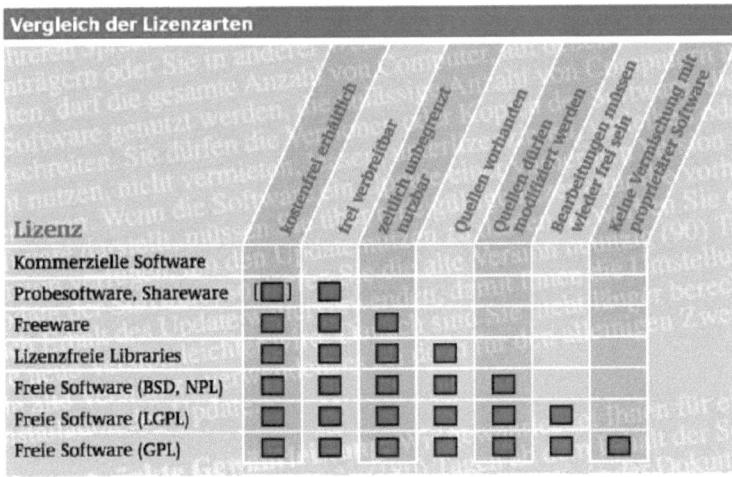

Vergleich der Lizenzarten							
Lizenz	kostenfrei erhältlich	frei verbreitbar	zeitlich unbegrenzt nutzbar	Quellen vorhanden	Quellen dürfen modifiziert werden	Bearbeitungen müssen wieder frei sein	keine Vermischung mit proprietärer Software
Kommerzielle Software							
Probesoftware, Shareware	[☐]	☐					
Freeware	☐	☐	☐				
Lizenzfreie Libraries	☐	☐	☐	☐			
Freie Software (BSD, NPL)	☐	☐	☐	☐	☐		
Freie Software (LGPL)	☐	☐	☐	☐	☐	☐	
Freie Software (GPL)	☐	☐	☐	☐	☐	☐	☐

Quelle: Siepmann, Jürgen: Freie Software – Rechtsfreier Raum?, Rechtssicherheit im Umgang mit Open Source Software. LinuxLand International, München, 2000.

Figure 1: Licenses and what they provide

5 Examples

Contrary to the past, there exits many Open Source solutions today. The already mentioned organization BerliOS or Sourceforge.org help publishing and finding OSS. Below you can see most popular examples for often used Open Source Software.

Anwendungsbeispiele		
Sparte	Open-Source-Software	Proprietäre Software, die auf OSS läuft
Warenwirtschaft & Rechnungswesen	kein für den professionellen Einsatz geeignetes System verfügbar	Parity [1], Abas-EKS [2]
Office	KOffice [3], StarOffice [4]	ApplixWare [5], Word Perfect [6]
Datenbanken	MySQL [7], PostgreSQL [8], InterBase [9]	Oracle [10], Informix [11], Adabas [12]

Figure 2: Examples for sucessful Open Source projects

Now, I'd like to present three project examples and one for a cost arithmetic.

5.1 Unix

UNIX was developed in 1969 as a multi-user and multi-tasking operating system for computers in the publicly regulated telephone company AT&T in the USA by Dennis Ritchie and Ken Thompson (Bell Laboratories).
Universities and research institutes asked if they could be part of the UNIX project; they were given the entire source code for a low price - after all, AT&T could only benefit from the contributions of the scientists. But increasingly restrictive AT&T licenses inspired others to own developments and work. Today there exist several derivatives:

- Darwin (2000, Apple)

- Solaris (1992, Sun Microsystems)

- Minix (1987, Vrije University Amsterdam)

- HP-UX (1986, Hewlett-Packard)

- Unicos 1.0 (1984, Cray Supercomputers)

- Sinix (1983, Siemens)

- XENIX OS (1980, Microsoft)

- BSD (1977, Berkeley University)

Different universities and almost every famous company from the computer branch, developed its own Unix derivate and thus produced huge competition.

5.2   GNU

The term GNU is an acronym for "GNU's Not UNIX". This term came from developer Richard Stallman.
Stallman's program package was conceived right from the outset as a replacement for UNIX from AT&T. At the start of the 1990s all the important components of GNU were complete; all that was missing was the Kernel, the stable operating system core. Linus Torvalds programmed a free UNIX kernel completely independently of Stallman's projects. This complemented the GNU system and made it a complete operating system.
Stallman has worked on developing GNU since 1983; he did not want to give up his copyrights to the programs - as if he had done so he would have opened up opportunities for other developers to modify his work and then sell it as their own product. Stallman provided the software he developed under the GNU General Public Licence (GPL).
In a Newsnet article Stallmann explained why he developed GNU:

"Why I Must Write GNU:
I consider that the golden rule requires that if I like a program I must share it with other people who like it. I cannot in good conscience sign a nondisclosure agreement or a software license agreement.
So that I can continue to use computers without violating my principles, I have decided to put together a sufficient body of free software so that I will be able to get along without any software that is not free."

Still today devotees of GNU insist on the term free software because of their ideological attitude.

5.3   Linux

Linux is a free, UNIX-like operating system, which originated in 1991 at Helsinki University. It was developed by Finnish student Linus Torvalds and then was placed under the GPL, the GNU General Public Licence. Thus Linux can be freely distributed, used and further developed.

Linux' father had the most power over the project. He decided which changes are useful and which are not. Developers could't really work autonomous. This fact and even cult of personality violates OSS principles as said in Open Source Definition.

In fact Linux is only the kernel of the operating system, which takes over data and storage administration and several low-level functions. Other important components, such as large sections of the operating system, the graphical user interface, parts of the network software and developer tools all came from GNU projects. All in all they make up the complete operating system GNU/Linux. The initial project was splitting in several projects and several distributors. Red Hat, SuSE, Caldera, Debian, Corel and Mandrake are amongst the best known; they combine and sell Linux with other free software and documentation. They have all agreed on one common standard (Linux Standard Base). But unfortunately the most distributions don't provide compatibility with the other projects.

5.4 Costs Example

The regional capital Munich organized the project "Client Survey". The aim was the comparison between costs for adapting and upgrading commercial and open source software and thus finding the most low priced operation system for a total of 14.000 computers.

For an period of 5 years of using operation system commercial software should be preferred. The reason for this is mostly the missing adapting and training costs. First there exists more advantages for open source for an period of 10 years. If open source is used less then 10 years, the institution has to pay for higher costs for training courses and adapting of special hardware. So, for longer periods Linux based systems cause 50% less budget costs. [Int03]

As you can see, Open Source Software is not always more cheap than commercial software. Its usability has to be checked in every field of application.

6 Conclusion

Open Source Software definitely has an learning effect for Software development. Because of OSS we know that flexible kinds of work and distribution and user support via Internet are possible.

But what's missing is a rational evaluation of the high economic usefulness of software. As recently as everybody understand this usefulness, then much more will be invested in German software and more software will be developed needed by economy and community.

As seen in this paper, it's an utopia that quality of software appears only by attention of users. There are too many uncertainties that can can happen or not. And OS Software is too dependent on the sentiments, interests and social skills of mainly hobby programmers. Qualitative high software does not need to be expensive but not every OS Software fulfills every quality claim.

I admit that there will always be a interest in OSS and sure why not. Who really doesn't care for gratis software? And I'm sure that popularity and spread of OSS will keep growing with cooperative help of organizations like BerliOS or Sourceforge. But blind trust in OSS is not appropriate. You never know, who really does OSS. The user has to check himself if quality, functionality, support and documentation are suitable even if there exists several plugins or forums.

A very positive example for Open Source Software is OSCommerce. A project should fulfill its characteristics. So a company and thus economy also can make use of OSS.

References

[Ber05] BerliOS. *OSS Ein Leitfaden für kleine und mittlere Unternehmen*, 2005. zuletzt gesehen 17.01.2005.

[Bez99] Nikolai Bezroukov. *OSS Development as a special type of academic research*, 1999. zuletzt gesehen 15.11.2004.

[End00] Albert Endres. *Open Source und die die Zukunft der Software*, 2000.

[Gra02] Volker Grassmuck. *Freie Software - Zwischen Privat- und Gemeineigentum*. Bundeszentrale für politische Bildung, 2002. zuletzt gesehen 17.01.2005.

[hSI05] http://de.wikipedia.org/wiki/Open Source-Initiative. *Wikipedia - Die freie Enzyklopädie*, 2005. zuletzt gesehen 24.01.2005.

[htt05] http://opensource.berlios.de/docs/osd.pdf. *The Open Source Definition*, 2005. zuetzt gesehen 24.01.2005.

[Int03] UNILOG Integrata. *Client Studie der Landeshauptstadt München*, 2003.

[Koc04] Frank Koch. *Rechtsrisiko Open Source Software?*, 2004.

[Ray98] Eric S. Raymond. *Halloween Document I*, 1998.

[Ray99] Eric S. Raymond. *The Cathedral and the bazaar*, 1999.

[Spi03] Prof. Dr. Gerald Spindler. *Rechtsfragen der Open Source Software*, 2003. zuletzt gesehen 17.01.2005.